The Haiku Guide

To

Williamsburg

Other books by Sally Stiles
available through Amazon.com
and palehorsebooks.com

Crazeman in The Bottle
The Haiku Guide to the Inside Passage
Plunge! A memoir

The Haiku Guide

To

Williamsburg

Sally Stiles

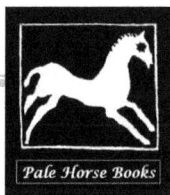

Pale Horse Books

Photographs by Sally Stiles

Library of Congress Control Number: 2016940615
ISBN 978-1-939917-18-8

Printed in
The United States of America

Pale Horse Books

www.palehorsebooks.com

musket fire
in the distance
Union Jack flinches

ides of March
only a sparrow
pauses to chat

tulips unfold
April garden
less formal

Gold Course
dogwood more impressive
than the score

redbuds—
swamp turtle blinks

after a squall
eavesdrop on
each birdhouse

Easter morning
fresh buds on
the burning bush

renewal—
even the pachysandra

with each gust
cherry tree bows
toward Buddha

long before
grapes are ripe
anticipation

James River beach:
memories cling
to bare toes

motorcycles thunder
into Yorktown
still the windmill

a thousand skies collide: distant storm

southern petticoats
sashay through town —
first wisteria

just beyond
the bridge
a bridge

Colonial Parkway
before tourists
buttercups

end of term
learned professor in his office
writing baseball books

day after graduation
so many paths
untaken

The Godspeed
docks in Jamestown—
400 years vanish

osprey defends
his nest
memorial day

summertime
puddles
to jump

Barnes & Noble
beach books where
grad gifts were

nibbling
cool mint leaves
Independence Day

peaceful afternoon
river paddling—
suddenly Busch Gardens

all we need to know—Grandpa's library

daybreak
pileated woodpecker
would peck wood

at the Muscarelle
DaVinci and Michelangelo
back to back

October first
shadows march
to a different drummer

first hint of autumn
an occasion
for inspiration

another stack
of white oak
daylight savings time

huzzah cloves,
carols, cressets:
Christmastide

holiday weekend
a dozen birds
left behind

twilight—
longing for
the gate to creak

deer tracks dimple
last night's snow
the year begins

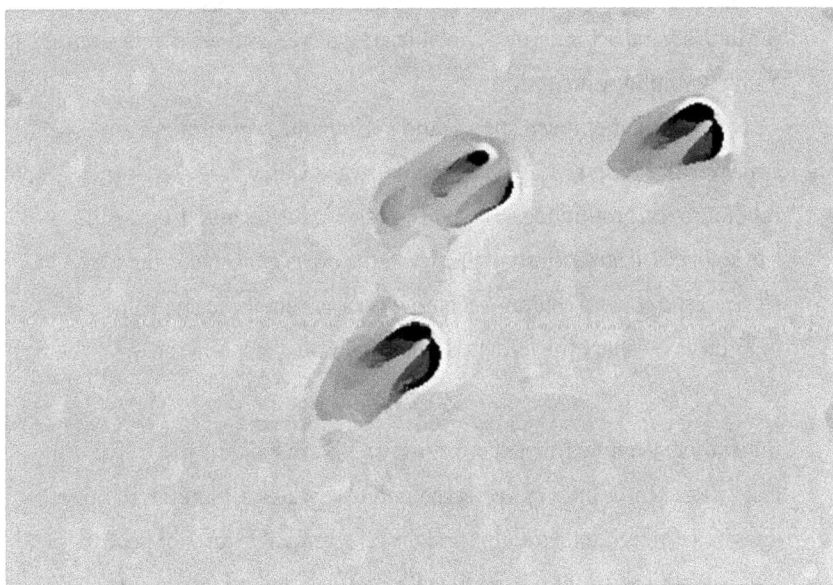

This book is a tribute to a remarkable place where, surprisingly, I have lived in one home for more years than ever before. I keep trying to leave to adventure elsewhere, but have been unsuccessful thus far. Perhaps Tidewater, Virginia, holds all the adventure I need, at least as long as some rural land meanders through it.

Besides being the home to significant historical sites and a living museum, at the heart of Williamsburg is the College of William & Mary, several art museums, notable art galleries and art events; even a small symphony orchestra.

Trees soar out of green spaces, and spring and summer flowers appear with exuberance. I share my backyard with wildlife—deer, rabbits, foxes, groundhogs, raccoons, possum, turtles and frogs, endless squirrels, lizards, dragon flies, even the occasional snake. Birds of all sizes, shapes and colors—eagles, hawks, cardinals, towhees, hummingbirds —share the feeders. I wouldn't have it any other way.

❖ ❖ ❖

Contrary to what we learned in primary school, a haiku is not restricted to three lines of five, seven and five syllables, nor even to three lines or seventeen total syllables. Haiku is a venerable form of poetry, the earliest forms dating from the 13th century. Haiku records an observation or moment of awareness—an aha! moment.

Writing haiku is an exercise in observing—and appreciating— what we discover. The purpose of this book is to give the reader the gift of some of the haiku moments we can all experience in Williamsburg.

I am very grateful to John Conlee, Lee Alexander and Greg Lilly for their thoughtful, intelligent consideration and effective encouragement as I created this collection; to Phyllis Barber, once again, for her conscientious probing of the manuscript; to our children and our grandchildren for providing the best possible reasons for us to relocate in Williamsburg, and to the good people who work so hard to retain the quality of life we enjoy here.

A special thank you to Susan Kight for a perfect afternoon cruising the James River on her boat, and the chance to take the last few photographs to complete the book.

Also a thank you to compte de Grasse and his French fleet. If France hadn't come to our aid in the battle of Yorktown, we might still be paying an exorbitant tax on our tea, and America would still be colonial.

❖ ❖ ❖

As my late friend, Kit Fournier, wrote: "My understanding of myself ebbed and flowed with the particular tides of the sea I was swimming in." I tend to understand myself better when I allow myself to swim in a sea of haiku. —Sally Stiles

❖ ❖ ❖

A portion of the proceeds from this book will be donated to Literacy For Life, The College of William & Mary, Williamsburg.

www.ingramcontent.com/pod-product-compliance
Lightning Source LLC
Chambersburg PA
CBHW050603280326
41933CB00011B/1963